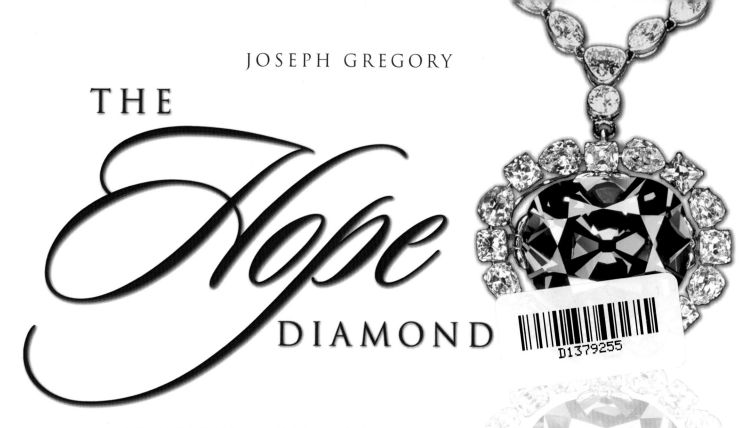

JOSEPH GREGORY

THE *Hope* DIAMOND

EVALYN WALSH MCLEAN AND THE CAPTIVATING
MYSTERY OF THE WORLD'S MOST ALLURING JEWEL

Providence House Publishers
WWW.PROVIDENCEHOUSE.COM
FRANKLIN, TENNESSEE

Printed in the United States of America

15   14   13   12   11   1   2   3   4   5

Library of Congress Control Number: 2010942933

ISBN: 978-1-57736-449-8

LeAnna Massingille *Cover and Page Designer*
Michele Thompson *Creative Consultant and Editorial Developer*

Cover image of the Hope diamond in its oval setting courtesy of the Smithsonian Institution © 2010—photo by Chip Clark

A Hillsboro Press Book

PROVIDENCE HOUSE PUBLISHERS
238 Seaboard Lane • Franklin, Tennessee 37067
www.providencehouse.com
800-321-5692

PREFACE

Evalyn Walsh McLean was a daughter, wife, mother, social worker, devoted friend, and owner of the Hope diamond—and she was my great-grandmother. I am deeply honored, with the publication of this commemorative gift book, to be able to share with you how the life of the world's most famous diamond intersected with the life of a most remarkable woman.

Of course, with Evalyn's death coming nearly twenty years before I was born, I never knew her personally. Over the years, however, I have been so blessed to learn of her extraordinary life. Whether through the numerous historical artifacts, personal memories of those who knew her, or the remembrances of her own children, I have come to cherish the life of Evalyn Walsh McLean both for the very public role she played throughout her life, and also for the less celebrated but more important role she played as the beloved matriarch of the Walsh-McLean family line.

As a member of that family line, I have the treasured gift of being custodian of a wonderful collection of various private heirlooms that elegantly chronicle the life of my great-grandmother. I am humbled and sometimes overwhelmed when I reflect upon the degree of history encompassed in this collection: family photos and portraits, magazine features and newspaper clippings about her life, her own newspaper columns and some of her personal correspondence, party registries and photo albums, and even some of her gowns.

Of the many treasures, one that I most cherish is the picture of my great-grandmother with my own mother, taken shortly before Evalyn's death in 1947. In it I find the heart of a woman who wore wealth around her neck, but knew instinctively where her eyes should be focused. I feel a strong connection to that heart.

In honoring the life of my great-grandmother, I also want to acknowledge and honor the life of Evalyn (Evie) Walsh McLean Reynolds, my grandmother, and to offer grateful testimony to the heritage she gave to me. As the baby in Evalyn's arms, my mother has missed the blessing that so many take for granted, in that both her grandmother, Evalyn, and her own mother, Evie, died while she was still very young. Fortunately, she has the numerous pictures and stories that keep her memories alive—when, for example, she would stay the weekend with Evalyn, my mother would play with the diamond in the sandbox. She is also known to have teethed on it and to have slept wearing it, while lying next to her grandmother.

Evalyn's generosity displayed itself time and again, and was especially appreciated when she would visit the wounded soldiers at Walter Reed Hospital, even allowing them, as they lay in their hospital beds, to play catch with the Hope. She was remarkably down to earth. Her idea of fun was shooting craps at a local police station, as her Great Dane, Mike, guarded the diamond by wearing it around his neck—not your typical dog collar.

Indeed, Evalyn was a grand socialite. As I reflect on her life, however, I am struck by the depth of her love for her family, her dedication to charitable interests, to those who sacrificed for our country, and to the down and out, in general. All of this stemmed from her undeniable and genuine love for people.

As you read through this book and come to see how the Hope diamond's history intersected with my family history, I hope that you will also be inspired by the life and the words of my great-grandmother—a woman who had great wealth and fame, but who came to know what holds true value in life.

This beautiful retelling of her story and her extraordinary journey would not have been possible without the great team effort of so many people. Thank you to Kathrine Currey for providing several of the images necessary for this book; to LeAnna Massingille whose talent is displayed in this wonderfully creative layout and cover; to Michele Thompson for her close collaboration in the researching, writing, and development of the narrative; and to Andrew Miller, my publisher and friend, thank you for your commitment to seeing Evalyn's story come to life in such a unique presentation for others to know and enjoy.

I am indebted to Richard Kurin, of the Smithsonian Institution, whose seminal work on the Hope diamond was an invaluable resource for this project. His assistance in confirming the factual accuracy of this story was greatly appreciated. I would also like to thank Randall Kremer and Kelly Carnes, who were instrumental in helping to secure the Smithsonian images needed to make this book complete.

Finally, I would like to dedicate this book to the memory of Carol Ann Rapp. On June 15th 2010, my dear friend, mentor, and greatest cheerleader, passed away. It was her constant encouragement and confidence in me that fortified my spirit to press ahead in my desire to rediscover my family's history, and then to share that history with you. Carol Ann was a collaborator on our earlier book, *Queen of Diamonds*, and we shared a great love and admiration for Evalyn and desired to see her legacy continued. She was excited and encouraged me, as I told her of the development of this newest book. I know she would be proud of its completed perfection.

I have always loved reading the words of my great-grandmother and trust that you will also. Throughout the book, designated in blue—type or background—are several quotes from her various writings. When people would leave Evalyn's home, "Friendship," she would always say to them, "Never say, 'Goodbye.' Always say, 'I'll see you later.'"

Joseph Gregory

I have my own little secret...

I HAD IT BLESSED MYSELF AND
I AM SITTING BACK ON THE
SIDE LINES LETTING THE CURSE
AND THE BLESSING FIGHT IT
OUT TOGETHER.

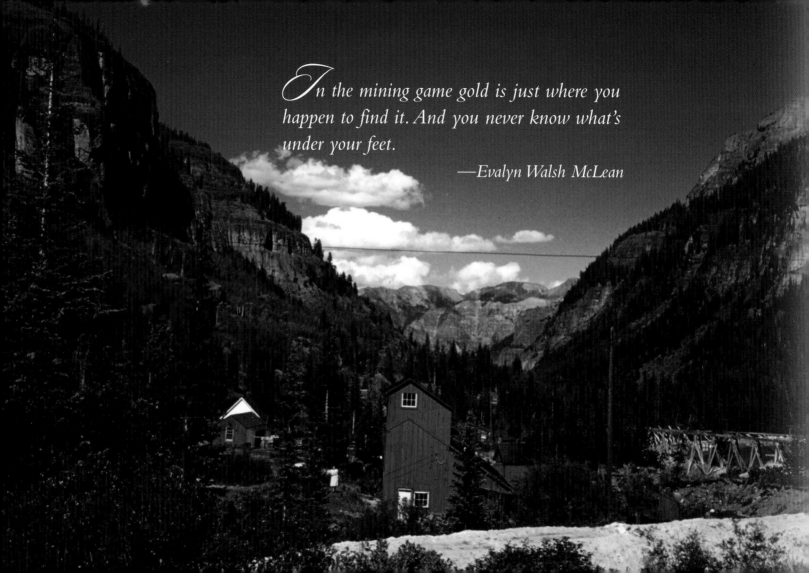

In the mining game gold is just where you happen to find it. And you never know what's under your feet.

—*Evalyn Walsh McLean*

STRIKING IT RICH

Mining fever is an illness that has afflicted untold numbers of people over the years. In the mid-1800s, in the newly established western towns of Colorado, a man by the name of Thomas Walsh had become incurably infected with this disease.

An Irishman from Tipperary, Tom Walsh had immigrated to the United States in 1869, moved to Colorado two years later, while working on the railroads, and shortly afterward contracted the "fever."

For twenty years he honed his trade, learned the ways of earth's creations, endured the hardships of an untamed Mother Nature, encountered economic obstacles and overcame them, fell victim to the battles of the mind and the body, but rose again—always looking, always testing, always learning, ever patient. He trained himself for success.

In June of 1896, his training paid off.

Having returned from a recent exploration, and being ill with a real fever, Walsh beckoned his ten-year-old daughter to his bedside and whispered the secret that would change their lives from that point on: "Daughter, I've struck it rich."

Though this change was not immediate, it was irrevocably decided.

Within a short period of time, the Walsh mine—Camp Bird Mine—was producing $5,000 a day.

With this newfound wealth, Tom Walsh decided to move his family to another little town where many who had found recent fortune were quickly settling. In 1897, the Walshes stepped into the bustling social scene of wealth and power in Washington, D.C.

I never have forgotten the excitement of our first winter in Washington. Every single thing we did was an adventure that gave us some fresh revelation of the meaning of the Camp Bird Mine.

This move quickly propelled the Walsh family, and especially Tom Walsh, to a place of great prominence. Evalyn's father seemed as at home in the midst of Washington's political and social action as he was quietly contemplating the line of a vein in a deserted mine. It was not long before governors, dignitaries, and presidents were hobnobbing with this farm boy from Ireland. Walsh was known for his ingenuity, his intelligence, his generosity, his integrity, and his *money*.

With this money, he freely lavished his family with extravagance. Those who dealt in the trade of extravagance knew well the name of Tom Walsh. One of those dealers was a certain jeweler by the name of Cartier.

By the summer of 1908, Evalyn Walsh had become Evalyn Walsh McLean, upon her marriage to an equally wealthy young man named Edward "Ned" McLean. Ned was the son of John R.

McLean (*pictured right*), owner of the *Washington Post* and the *Cincinnati Enquirer*, and for whom McLean, Virginia is named. Between the wealth of both fathers, this young couple had financial opportunities that very few ever have. Their honeymoon, for example, included stops in Amsterdam, Germany, France, and Turkey (*pictured left*).

Another opportunity came in 1910 when Pierre Cartier paid them a visit at their hotel in Paris. Being the salesman that he was and knowing his client well, Cartier proceeded to intrigue Mrs. McLean with a tale that wove into the tapestry of history threads of both fact and fiction, captivating his audience with mystery, drama, deceit, revolution, and an ancient curse.

With Evalyn's interest piqued, he carefully opened an elegantly wrapped package and presented to this daughter of Tom Walsh that gem of which she would soon become the new owner—the famed Hope diamond. Although Evalyn turned down his offer on account of not liking its setting, Cartier did not give up easily. Soon after their

*P*ierre Cartier came to call on us at the Hotel Bristol in Paris. He carried, tenderly, a package tightly closed with wax seals. His manner was exquisitely mysterious. I suppose a Parisian jewel merchant who seeks to trade among the ultra-rich has to be more or less a stage manager and an actor. Certainly he must be one great salesman.

return to the States, Cartier again paid them a visit. He now presented the diamond in a striking new setting. This one, she liked.

For more than thirty five years, Evalyn Walsh McLean unashamedly courted this jewel around town, around the house, and around the world. This miner's daughter turned socialite has become, over the years, synonymous with the diamond. It was while under her ownership that much of the popular swell of myth and mystery surrounding the Hope took on a life of its own, and much of that by Mrs. McLean's own making.

AN IDOL'S CURSE AND TAVERNIER'S VIOLET

The true story of this jewel is indeed one of mystery, drama, deceit, and revolution. For nearly four hundred years, the life and journey of this diamond has been documented. It has traveled from India, to France, to England, to America, and beyond. It has been

worn around the necks of kings, commoners, and even a Great Dane; it has been stolen and "rediscovered," pawned and reclaimed; it has undergone several name changes and taken on different looks; it has been the envy of royalty and thieves alike; and it has been witness to a remarkable history.

The story of this world traveler has intrigued far more imaginations than that of Evalyn McLean, and for good reason. The tale it has to tell is riveting.

But what about that curse? For an answer to that question, we must journey back to where it all began. It is widely believed that the Kollur Diamond Mine in India is the birthplace of what was then nothing but an obscure piece of earth. It would not stay that way for long.

In the seventeenth century, India was the only known producer of diamonds, and all those who sought success in this trade looked to India as the source of that success. From a very young age, Jean Baptiste Tavernier (*left*), a renowned French jewel merchant, had desired to be a world traveler. When he set sail, around the year 1642, Tavernier had no idea that he was about to step into the opening scene of a story for the ages. It was on that trip that he came into the possession of what would become his most famous prize.

Just how this event took place is not fully known, and it is in the absence of fact that myth was born. Legend has it, that the jewel was actually stolen from the eye of an idol worshipped by the followers of a Hindu god, some say the god Rama Sita. As a result of this alleged act, the story is told that the angered god, as a means of enacting vengeance, placed a curse on the robber and all of the diamond's subsequent owners.

So how did Tavernier come to possess this cursed gem?

It has been said that he was approached by a secretive slave, some say by a priest, who had a

SITA-RAMA
HEROINE OF THE RAMAYANA

"*You know about the Turkish Revolution?*" *said Cartier.*

"*Why,*" *I told him,* "*we were in Constantinople when there was shooting in the streets. We went there on our honeymoon. I was admitted to the Sultan's harem—just a lot of fatties, except for two or three who wore Worth gowns.*"

"*Ah, I do not forget such things. You told me when you bought from me your wedding present, the Star of the East. It seems to me you told me then that you had seen a jewel in the harem, a great blue stone that rested against the throat of the Sultan's favorite. A lovely throat, eh?*"

"*I guess I did.*" *It was too early to argue and, after all, I had seen jewels on Turkish ladies that made my fingers itch.*

"*Of course you did,*" *said Cartier.* "*Such things impress one.*"

"*It seems to me I did see that stone.*"

"*Naturally. We hear the woman who had that jewel from the Sultan's hand was stabbed to death.*"

All my boredom vanished as he went on.

business proposition for the traveler. Others say that Tavernier, himself, was the greedy culprit who brazenly removed the eye from the idol and stowed it away as his own.

A more likely scenario, as well as a factual one, is that Tavernier purchased this gem, and did so in a legal and acceptable manner.

Regardless of how it found its way into his hands, when he laid his eyes on this stone of 112 3/16 carats and radiating a hypnotizing steel blue, Tavernier knew what he was seeing— it was not a sapphire, as it could easily be mistaken to be. It was a diamond.

And, as we now know, it is the world's largest deep blue diamond.

Some twenty-six years later, in 1668, Tavernier smuggled the diamond to Paris, where he sold it to King Louis XIV, the Sun King —a self-proclaimed title, identifying himself with Apollo, the Greek god of the sun. King Louis invited Tavernier into his court to tell of his adventures. Louis XIV bought what was then known as the Tavernier Violet, along with well over one thousand other diamonds.

"Bad luck objects,"
I said to Cartier,
"for me are lucky."
"Ah, yes," he said.
"Madame told me that
before, and I remembered.
I think, myself, that
superstitions of the kind
we speak about are baseless.
Yet, one must admit,
they are amusing."

Because of Tavernier's good reputation as a jewel merchant, he was made a baron. With his new wealth, he purchased a large estate in Aubonne, Switzerland. At the time of his passing, Tavernier was eighty four years old and had lived a very full life, a fact which helps to dispel the myth of the curse. Even though there remains a strong rumor that Tavernier was found mauled to death by a pack of dogs, or wolves, there is no evidence for this and no actual information to indicate how he did die.

FRENCH ROYALTY AND
THE FRENCH BLUE

In 1673, King Louis XIV had the stone re-cut by the court jeweler, in order to enhance its beauty. The result of this action was a 67 1/8-carat stone, which then became known as the Blue Diamond of the Crown or, more commonly, the French Blue.

The cutting of the diamond served as a repudiation of the ancient Indian belief that the larger a diamond the more protection and power it afforded its owner. To cut away at a diamond was done for the purpose of ridding it of flaws. To reduce the size too dramatically would not only limit the power of the diamond, but could also invite in sorrow—or what might be interpreted by some as a curse.

For the Sun King, however, sparkle was much more important than size. As a great supporter of the arts and the commissioner of Versailles, style was of the

utmost importance to Louis, and diamonds were a big part of that—lots of diamonds. King Louis XIV bedecked himself and all things around him in elegance and extravagance in the extreme. It is no wonder, then, that Tavernier, the blessed deliverer of diamonds, was so honored by the king.

In 1715, at seventy-seven years of age, King Louis XIV died. His five-year-old great-grandson and successor to the throne inherited not only a powerful country, but also a love for diamonds and extravagance, and he found his own stunning ways to display that love.

As a means of expressing his loyalty to his heritage, Louis XV, in 1749, had the stone reset into a piece of ceremonial jewelry for the Order of the Golden Fleece. This piece of jewelry, celebrating one's induction into a relatively elite club of aristocracy and royalty, was only worn by the king.

In an attempt to elevate himself amongst European royalty, Louis purposefully enhanced the rather colorless Order with hundreds of diamonds featuring, of course, the French Blue.

A royal legacy was being established among these French leaders. Louis XVI was also inducted into the Order of the Golden Fleece, thus inheriting the brilliant version that Louis XV had created.

However, although King Louis XVI, along with the queen Marie Antoinette, had inherited a love of extravagance, they were not blessed with a thriving country. France was undergoing quite dramatic social changes. The leadership of the king, which did not reflect those changes, was lacking in effectiveness.

Statements such as Antoinette's, "Let them eat cake," did not endear the queen to the commoners of her country. The flamboyance of their wealth was clearly visible for their struggling countrymen to witness. They didn't like it.

The 1789 storming of the Bastille (*page 28, bottom*) was reflective of the discontent that was rampant within the underprivileged class in France. The old aristocratic guard seemed to be falling. When a mob attacked Versailles Palace, Louis and the queen were evacuated to the Palais des Tuileries for safekeeping, becoming virtual prisoners.

I might have been excused, that morning, for believing that all the violences of the French Revolution were just the repercussions of that Hindu idol's wrath. M. Cartier was most entertaining.

In 1791, with the violence of the Revolution in full swing and threatening their lives, these two prisoners made an attempt to flee France, but were unsuccessful. With their capture, the French Crown Jewels, including the French Blue, were confiscated and placed in the Garde-Meuble, a sort of royal warehouse.

Louis and Marie were placed in royal lockdown. And, in 1793, Louis XVI and Marie Antoinette were sent to the guillotine.

Diamonds have a strong fascination for people. They always have had and always will have, and at least they are like your dog —they never turn on you, never answer you back, and they always stick with you, unless a robber comes in through the window or you have to pawn them.

REVOLUTION AND
CONSPIRACY THEORIES

France was in a state of tremendous turmoil—socially, financially, diplomatically. Various factions were competing for control. As a means of trying to regain some economic standing, it was suggested that the Crown Jewels be sold, and plans were being made to do so.

It was about this time that one of the greatest heists in history took place.

In September 1792, the Garde-Meuble was robbed several times. On the night of September 16, several men were observed by a member of the National Guard looting the Royal Warehouse. Although a few were caught, most got away, and most of the jewels with them. Among the jewels that were stolen were the Regent, the Sancy, and the Order of the Golden Fleece. Although some of the jewels were

recovered, the French Blue was not. It is generally agreed that the Golden Fleece was broken up and sold for its parts.

Enormous speculation has surrounded this event, even to this day.

Some say that Marie Antoinette is to blame, and that she was conspiring from the place of her confinement to regain the jewels that she might procure the funds to purchase her release from prison. Some are convinced that it was a plot to overthrow the government by one of the competing factions.

It has been speculated that the diamond was sold to the Spanish royal family. As proof for this theory, a 1799 Goya portrait of Maria Luisa of Spain (*right*) is often cited as evidence. It shows Maria Luisa wearing a necklace with a large blue stone in the center. Close examination, however, reveals a stone that appears noticeably larger than the Hope. Since virtually all other stories place the diamond in England during this time, ownership of the diamond by Spanish royalty is doubtful.

A less intriguing theory is that the guards at the Royal Warehouse were simply inept in their duty, and that this great theft was a prime

example of the looting that takes place in the midst of chaotic times. Of all the conspiratorial views of the event, proponents of the overthrow theory seem to have a fascinating case.

In 1792, the Austrian Carl Wilhelm Ferdinand, Duke of Brunswick, was chosen by the leaders of Prussia and Austria to lead the counter-resistance against the Revolutionaries. It is contended that Carl was bribed by some leaders of the French Revolution for the purpose of securing a victory. In exchange for basically throwing the fight, which in this case was the key battle at Valmy (*shown on pages 34–35*), Duke Ferdinand is purported to have received a certain blue diamond, one which was formally a member of the French Crown Jewels.

While it is true that the Revolutionaries won the battle against the Prussia-Austria alliance, that outcome is more likely the result of errors in strategy and issues of control amongst the military leaders, rather than the ingenious plotting of an evil cabal. Still, the case is compelling and it doesn't end there.

CAROLINE, NAPOLEON, AND THE PRINCE REGENT GEORGE

Upon the conclusion of the battle at Valmy, the Duke of Brunswick returned home to his daughter, Caroline Amelia, and to his wife, Augusta Hanover, who happened to be the older sister of King George III of Great Britain (*right*).

The king of England was facing his own battles, many of which were with his son, George, the Prince of Wales. Duke Carl Wilhelm and Duchess Augusta, at the same time, were having an equally difficult time with their daughter, the cousin of Prince George.

A strategy for the home front was arranged between the sister and the brother, the plan of which was to unite their two problem children into holy matrimony, thus bringing about a sense of order and stability in their wayward lives. The strategy, like that of Valmy, was not successful.

The Mother Red-Cap Public House, in opposition, to the King's Head.

Prince George and Caroline (*right*) did not get along, to say the least. In spite of this fact, they were somehow able to produce a daughter, Charlotte, who was born on January 7, 1796. It did not go unnoticed that this date was exactly nine months after their wedding ceremony on April 8, 1795. Once again, speculation enters the picture. It is asserted that Caroline, who had several male friends, was perhaps already impregnated prior to the wedding.

These wild royals were soon publicly estranged, living in separate quarters. All the while George maintained his bachelor ways, and Caroline frequently "entertained" her male friends, claiming to the end of her life the innocence of these friendships. The scandal between the two was common fodder for the public, the press, and cartoonists of the day.

In the meantime, Napoleon had gained power in France. In 1806, he and his armies had defeated the Austrian duke, taken possession of his territory, and confiscated all the treasures of the Brunswick Palace. Augusta Hanover and her son Frederick William escaped to

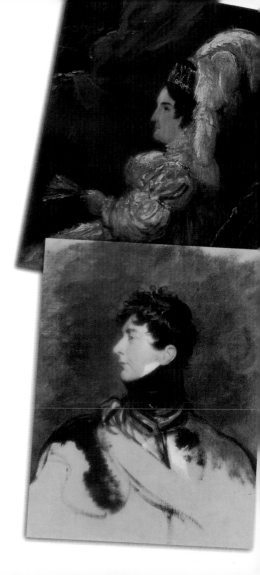

England, where they sought shelter with her brother, George III. But Napoleon, in taking those treasures, was looking to restore French honor, and that in part by regaining the Crown Jewels.

Knowing this, and assuming that he ever had the French Blue, the duke may have had the diamond cut down yet again sometime prior to his 1806 defeat, in an attempt to disguise it as something other than what Napoleon (*left*) could claim as state property. An 1806 painting of Caroline wearing a gemstone necklace of eerie similarity to the French Blue is often used as evidence to advance this theory.

How or why Caroline would be in possession of a possibly re-cut French Blue is not known. However, this is not a wholly implausible scenario. If the duke was trying to keep the Blue out of Napoleon's hands, it seems likely that he would do more than just re-cut it. He would also send it to a relatively safe place—England, to be in the hands of a safe relative—Caroline.

In late 1806, Caroline's father, Duke Ferdinand, was killed in battle. With her family basically in exile and living on the good graces of George III, it was not an ideal time for Caroline to be at odds with her husband, but their relationship only continued to worsen. Caroline was ostracized and was kept nearly entirely from seeing their daughter Charlotte. Caroline's circumstances were becoming rather precarious, and her financial options limited.

In September of 1812, there was a legal memorandum in which a large blue diamond, of approximately 45-carats, was documented by an English jeweler, John Francillon. In this report, the ownership of the diamond is attributed to a man named Daniel Eliason, a London diamond merchant.

It is speculated that at some point between 1810 and 1812, Caroline secretly sold the version of the French Blue which her father had supposedly given her to Eliason in an attempt to alleviate her financial burdens.

The 1812 sale date fits nicely into the legal order, passed during the reign of Napoleon, which set the statute of limitations for any crimes committed during wartime at twenty years, allowing for the

reemergence of the diamond, re-cut or not, to take place without criminality accorded it. Was this Eliason's plan? Who knows? What is known is that our traveling diamond, for a period of time, ended up in the hands of one Daniel Eliason.

By 1815, the war that England had been waging with France ended; Napoleon conceded defeat. With this news, great celebration took place throughout Europe (most of which had joined together to oppose Napoleon), as did a reinstatement of order. England's Prince, now Prince Regent George, began a renewed and very congenial diplomacy with the new leader of France—King Louis XVIII. George was flying high.

His daughter Charlotte's sudden death in 1817 only exacerbated the already strained relationship between he and Caroline. Soon after this event, George's vindictive campaign to have Caroline tried for

I kid myself, of course —but I like to pretend the thing brings good luck. As a matter of fact, the luckiest thing about it is that, if I ever had to, I could hock it.

adultery, and ultimately witchcraft, in the public court left Caroline teetering on a very high precipice.

The death of the long-infirm King George III in 1820 brought about additional order, at least in the eyes of the Prince Regent George, who now would accede to the throne. An inheritance of freedom was bestowed upon George with the passing of his father. With this freedom, George's attacks on Caroline increased, as did his love for ornamentation—of every kind possible. Enter Tavernier's little diamond from India. No bill or receipt of purchase has ever been found, but somewhere around the year 1823, George IV took possession of a stolen prize.

Did he know the details of this diamond's journey, or was it simply a striking addition to his collection about which he could boast? Did he know Caroline had pawned this jewel so that she might have more leverage to withstand his attacks? He must have had his suspicions, even if he had no evidence. Still, circumstantial evidence and rumor alone, along with the satisfaction he must have felt to have outmaneuvered both Caroline and Napoleon, is more than enough to solidify in his mind what might or might not be true. King George IV did not pass up an opportunity to glory in his own success—real or perceived.

In August of 1821, a very disheartened Caroline (*right*) died. That next year, Sir Thomas Lawrence was commissioned to paint a portrait of the newly enthroned king. Of the regalia which George sports in that portrait, one blue stone has created quite a stir among historians and curious people in general. He appears to be wearing the very diamond, in the exact cut, of what is now so popularly known to us as the Hope diamond.

If he truly was the owner of this storied diamond, and knew so, why didn't he just come right out and say? Well, it was a stolen diamond, and one stolen from the country of his good friend King Louis XVIII. If it were common knowledge that his new diamond was one that he not only wanted to keep from Napoleon, but from everyone, that might create a bit of strain in his relationship with France's leader—and George seemed finally to be at a place where

he was free of his strained relationships. Surely, more bad press was not what he wanted. Plus, he liked the diamond.

With the death of George IV (*at right*) in 1830, a new era began for our diamond. His successor, William IV, upon assessing the extent of George's debt and understanding the mood of the country toward the royal family—George's abuse of the Treasury amidst the poverty of much of the citizenry is depicted in the cartoon at left—chose to sell much of George's jewels as quietly and as quickly as possible.

THE HOPE FAMILY AND A NEW NAME

One option for William was to turn to the Hopes of London. The Hopes, a prominent banking family, had some influence over and were well known by a number of national government leaders, including those of Russia, Sweden, Spain, Portugal, and the United States. It was their company, along with Baring of

London, who made the loan to the United States to finance the Louisiana Purchase.

Henry Hope (*top left*), along with his uncles and cousin, had generated millions for Hope & Company and ultimately for the entire family. Although the company was no longer in operation, its sale to Baring of London in 1813 had brought a great deal of wealth to the heirs of that banking legacy. Henry Philip Hope (*bottom left*) was one of those great beneficiaries, and it is at this point in history where the diamond takes on the name by which it is so popularly identified today.

An 1839 catalogue entry of Hope's gem collection indicates a beautifully unique, large blue diamond. No mention is made regarding from where it was purchased, or from whom. However, Henry Philip Hope would had to have known about the French Blue and its history. It is possible that he meant to not mention the diamond's history. Doing so may have put him in the same position

No other gem I know of is so rare as a real blue diamond; I have never seen another the precise blue of the Hope Diamond. The blue of it is something I am puzzled to name. Peking blue would be too dark, West Point blue too grey. A Hussar's coat? Delft? A harbor blue? Sometimes when I have looked at it, I have felt that Nature, when making it, was half inclined to form a sapphire, but its diamond hardness dispels that thought, and, really, it has no more than a quarter of the blue of soft sapphires.

That very rareness of color is the thing that convinced me the Hope and Brunswick were once a single treasure

that George IV had been in; recognition could have delegitimized his ownership of the gem.

The same year of the catalog entry, Henry Philip Hope died. As he had never married, nor had any children of his own, his inheritance was to be split between his three nephews. A lengthy court battle between the brothers quickly ensued and, in the end, it was Henry Thomas Hope who was the victor. As his ownership of the diamond came around the same time as the 1851 Great Exhibition of London at the Crystal Palace, he lent it for a time to be on display.

Prior to its exhibition, however, the then Duke of Brunswick, Charles, requested a private viewing of the Hope. This nephew of Queen Caroline and grandson of Carl Wilhelm Ferdinand believed there was a connection to be made to the 67 1/8-carat French Blue. Was this Hope diamond cut from the French Blue and a part of his family's history? Although Charles did view the diamond, and may have believed the two were one in the same, it does not appear that he attempted to use this knowledge against Hope in any way.

In 1877, gemologist Edwin Streeter in his book *Precious Stones and Gems* contended that the Hope could quite possibly have been cleaved from the French Blue, with the qualifier that the two would have to be identical in color. Streeter's examination and research concludes that there are actually three stones, of distinct size but identical color, which found their origin in the French Blue—the Hope, the Brunswick Blue, and the smallest, the Pirie.

The Brunswick Blue, which probably came from the Brunswick holdings and weighing in at 13 carats, is what Charles of Brunswick would have had with him when he paid a visit to Mr. Hope. If he did, in fact, believe that his Blue and the Hope were sister stones, why not speak up? Well, such evidence could only substantiate the rumors of Valmy, validating the allegation of treachery against his grandfather (*left*), thus bringing shame upon his family name.

It would seem a simple solution to gather the three stones in one place and allow modern-day science to solve the mystery. Unfortunately, the whereabouts of the Brunswick and the Pirie are not known. And so, as is true with much of the Hope's history, rumor, myth, and allegation have the day.

As such, the story continues.

LORD FRANCIS, MAY YOHE, AND THE RELEASE OF THE HOPE'S DIAMOND

In 1861, Henry Thomas Hope's daughter, Henrietta, married Henry Pelham-Clinton, Earl of Lincoln, whose excessive gambling debts had driven him from his home country and who was not the most upright of character. Upon the Earl's marriage to Henrietta, his debts were settled and he and Henrietta were given a yearly stipend on which to live. When Henry Thomas died in 1862, his wife Anne Adele inherited the gem. Greatly concerned that her son-in-law's costly gambling habit might cause him to sell the Hope family properties, her will made certain stipulations to prevent such actions.

*T*here are those who would believe that somehow a curse is housed deep in the blue of the Hope Diamond. I scoff at that in the privacy of my mind, for I do comprehend the source of what is evil in our lives; but I can see no way to filter out the blackness from the magic that oppresses us. The hamperings I wish to overcome are, I think, the natural consequences of unearned wealth in undisciplined hands.

Upon Adele's death in 1884, the entire Hope estate was passed along to Henrietta's younger son, Henry Francis. This was done on two conditions: that he change his surname to Hope and that the inheritance would only be granted as a "life interest," meaning that he was restricted in his freedom to sell any part of his inheritance without court approval. In 1887, the now Lord Francis Hope, received his inheritance.

Lord Francis, an apparent chip off the old block, was forever in debt. As a result, many years were spent in litigation with his siblings who strongly opposed the selling off of the family's wealth in order to alleviate his financial burden. He filed for bankruptcy, and in 1896 it was discharged. Still, he was unsuccessful in his court battles against his family, unable to sell the Hope diamond. Under such a weight, Lord Francis was basically supported by his wife, May Yohe (*right*), his mistress whom he had married in 1894.

May was a free-spirited, passionate actress, made famous equally by her talents as a star of the stage, as well as her much

For hours that jewel stared at me. The setting had been changed completely to a frame of diamonds, and there was a splendid chain of diamonds to go about my neck. At some point during that night I began to want the thing.

publicized exploits—her marriage to Lord Francis being one of these.

Billing herself as Lady Francis, she often made claims to elevate her standing, including claims to have worn the Hope diamond that were later to be contradicted by Lord Francis and others. She seems to have transferred the fanciful world of the stage onto her much disappointed reality.

Even after Lord Francis's bankruptcy had been discharged, he continued to habitually spend money that he did not have, with a new mountain of debt rising.

In 1900, May's disappointment found refuge in Captain Putnam Bradlee Strong. By the early part of 1901, May and Captain Strong had run off together. Lord Francis was now alone and still in great need of money. He made another attempt at gaining permission to sell the Hope. This time, the family relented.

For May Yohe, she appears to have reaped what she sowed. Captain Strong had an affair, according to May, and sold off all of her jewelry.

Their marriage dissolved shortly thereafter. Yohe made a successful comeback in the London production of *Little Christopher Columbus*, often wearing a replica of the Hope diamond throughout the run of the show.

A new surge of popularity began to occur in the life of our legendary diamond, beginning with a 1908 newspaper article, continuing off and on over the next few years, and certainly upon the purchase of the diamond by Mr. and Mrs. McLean. May Yohe, seeing the opportunity before her, once again turned to her outstanding imagination and bent toward hyperbole.

In 1921, Yohe found success with her book, *The Mystery of the Hope Diamond,* as well as a silent film series called "The Hope Diamond Mystery." Taking the already mythical accounts of the diamond and incorporating her own exaggerated life experiences, this film series more than pushed the envelope with regard to artistic license. It is in this series where May wholeheartedly begins to ride

the wave of the cursed jewel, blaming all of her life's woes on her proximity to the diamond.

The non-staged reality of her life, however, scripted that she continue performing, because that income was needed to support herself and her new husband, disabled veteran John Smuts. Toward the end of her life, the harshness of the Depression found May mopping floors for the Works Progress Administration earning far, far less than in the glory of her former days.

The success of her book and her film series, however, have securely fixed her and her history into the ongoing tale of our main character.

As the year 1902 came to an end, that famed blue diamond of the legendary banking family was now released from Hope's familial care and began an eight year journey of relative unsettledness.

From the hands of Lord Francis, the Hope made its way next into the possession of Joseph Frankel's Sons and

Company, a New York jewelry firm. Unfortunately, by the beginning of 1908 Frankel's Sons was experiencing what a number of the diamond's previous and future owners would also experience —financial hardship. To whom would our diamond now go?

FROM THE HOPES TO THE MCLEANS

A wealthy Turkish diamond collector and merchant named Selim Habib was the next owner. Did he purchase it on behalf of Abdul Hamid II, the Sultan of Turkey? Some believe so. This would certainly comport with the tale Pierre Cartier told to Evalyn regarding her visit to the Sultan's harem on her honeymoon. Once again, there is no evidence to truly support this claim, except that Cartier planted the thought in Evalyn's head to help her remember what she probably never actually saw. To the contrary, Habib's sales records specify that the Sultan never owned the Hope. What is known is that Habib also found himself in financial straits. So, once again, in 1909, our jewel was sold.

Every day I received letters from persons near and far who had read that I had become the owner of this stone. I had letter after letter from May Yohe, now trying to recoup some bit of happiness from the ruin of her life. She blamed the diamond; . . . she begged me to throw it away and break its spell. . . . I began to have about my life some of that feeling with which we await the rising of a curtain at a play.

It was purchased by yet another jeweler, Simon Rosenau, but it would not stay with him for long either. By 1910, when Ned and Evalyn McLean were vacationing in Paris, Cartier Jewelers owned this gem. Cartier had purchased it, but not with the intent of keeping it. Thus came Pierre's visit to the Hotel Bristol.

The Cartier's had been in business for more than sixty years. Begun by Louis-Francois Cartier, continued on by Alfred, and now under the shared leadership of brothers Jacques, Louis, and Pierre, this highly respected family was known by world leaders, members of aristocracy, and by the famous and wealthy. Ned and Evalyn McLean fit very well into those last two categories.

However, though Cartier knew of Evalyn's love of diamonds, the sale of this particular one was not a given, as evidenced by her earlier rejection of it. Pierre was quite familiar with the diamond's history, real and fictitious. He had heard the rumor mill grind out the tales of Tavernier's supposed misfortune and all the rumors of tragedy that surrounded the diamond's years with the French kings. The Revolution, the treachery at Valmy, George and Caroline, the Hopes, May Yohe, and several exaggerated, contrived news accounts that fed and perpetuated the myth were certainly all known by Mr. Cartier.

Had he chosen, he could also have threaded in accounts of Catherine the Great (*bottom right*) and her relationship to Henry Hope, her family's connection to the Brunswicks, and the possession of her own famous and intriguing diamond, the Orloff (*right*). He could have drawn on a whole host of stories of heartache that occurred to people because of their association with the diamond. From the mistreatment and banishment of Louis XIV's mistress, Madame de Montespan, to the imprisonment and death of Nicolas Fouquet (*top right*), to the brutal death by mob beating of Princess Lamballe, who was a

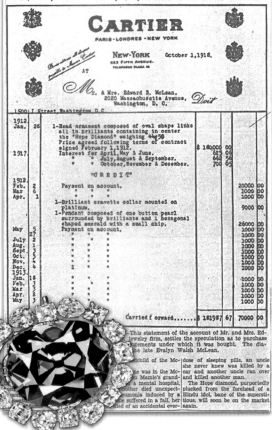

confidante of Marie Antoinette, the path of destruction appeared to be endless.

Surely, Cartier had heard it all. And with the McLeans he had shared it, a lot of it anyway. So what was it that sealed the deal? Well, while Evalyn was out one day Pierre simply dropped the diamond off, leaving it with Ned, so that it and Mrs. McLean could become better acquainted. Finally, in January 1911 the deal was sealed.

There was a significant dispute between Cartier and Ned McLean regarding the exact nature of the sale. Allegations and refutations went back and forth. A suit was filed. Claims were made, and countered. Eventually, an agreement was reached—Cartier was paid in dribs and drabs, and the McLeans kept the Hope diamond.

Oddly, after all the legal hassle involved in this exchange, there were no hard feelings. The relationship between the Cartiers and the McLeans remained friendly, not cursed.

*T*hen I signed a note and Ned signed too. I put the chain around my neck and thereby seemed to hook my life to its destiny of good or evil.

    I knew Ned's mother would try to stop me. That was why I hurried to make the purchase irrevocable. When Cartier had put our note inside his pocket, I called Mrs. McLean on the telephone.

    "Mummie, I have bought the Hope Diamond."

    What I heard her say was, "It is a cursed stone and you must send it back. Worse than its being freighted with bad luck is your buying of it—a piece of recklessness. Money is a trust for better things than jewel buying."

EVALYN WALSH MCLEAN
AND HER ALLURING DIAMOND

For good, bad, or otherwise, the next thirty-six years found Mrs. Ned McLean and her Hope to be nearly inseparable. Evalyn Walsh McLean lived anything but a normal, sedate, quiet life. Her entire life, in fact, was full of adventure, drama, and intrigue, either in reality or in the fancy of her young imaginative mind. Boredom, she said, was the thing she hated most. As a young girl, she had watched her family struggle in the rough and tumble ways of the western mining towns. She had seen, even by the age of ten, plenty of ups and downs; she and her family had experienced close calls and heartache; and she had watched her father work himself to near death.

But the Walshes were a stubborn, vivacious, hard working clan, full of hopes and dreams. Their tenacity bore itself out in nearly everything they put their hands and

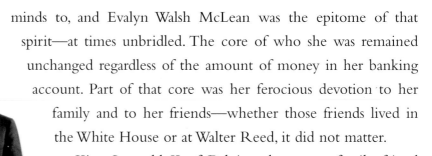

minds to, and Evalyn Walsh McLean was the epitome of that spirit—at times unbridled. The core of who she was remained unchanged regardless of the amount of money in her banking account. Part of that core was her ferocious devotion to her family and to her friends—whether those friends lived in the White House or at Walter Reed, it did not matter.

King Leopold II of Belgium became a family friend soon after Tom Walsh had begun amassing his fortune, during the time the Walshes were living in Paris. Upon their return to Washington, D.C., Mr. Walsh commissioned the construction of a new home, one that would be large enough to house a suite of rooms fit for a king—one very specific king. Affectionately referred to as "2020," this sixty room mansion on Massachusetts Avenue served as a more than able dwelling for the Walshes and played host to a great many social gatherings throughout the years. King Leopold, however, never did occupy his

Deep inside me, there was going on a chemistry I wish I fully understood. How ultra-wise I should be then! Yet I insist that every time I have been pregnant I have been presciently aware that I was engaged in the greatest of all magic. I? Perhaps I mean that God was doing this.

At any rate I knew that incomprehensible forces within my being were building up a human entity. What best of Ned, what best of me had been imparted to my child? I used to lie awake and ponder even as I felt the baby growing.

My child was born December 18, 1909, in 2020 Massachusetts Avenue, Vinson Walsh McLean. He was called in newspaper headlines "the hundred-million dollar baby," and if that was an exaggeration as to his prospects as an heir it seemed to me a gross understatement of his value. He had a golden crib, and in it he was sheltered from all draughts by a lacy, quilted canopy depending from an arrangement like a crown. This crib was a gift from King Leopold.

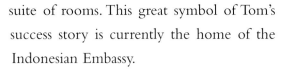

suite of rooms. This great symbol of Tom's success story is currently the home of the Indonesian Embassy.

Evalyn was passionate about everything and everyone she loved. That fiery spirit and tendency toward compassion was displayed time and again, whether in the extravagance of her famous parties, venturing out into a blizzard to help feed World War I veterans, entertaining GIs in her home and at charity events, or loaning her Hope diamond to young brides to wear at their wedding— serving as both something borrowed and something blue. Both 2020 and Friendship, another of Evalyn's residences, served throughout the years to house various war efforts and agencies such as the American Red Cross.

Be it Christmas, New Year's, Easter, Thanksgiving, or just a Saturday night, Evalyn was never at a loss for an occasion to throw a party. At home equally with wounded soldiers or D.C. elite, Mrs. McLean was always heavily adorned and ready to entertain. Her genuine kindness sparkled like the jewels she showcased. She was particularly loved by the veterans who were regular recipients of her hospitality, either as guests in her own home or when she brought the party to them at Walter Reed Hospital.

Perhaps her most well-known guests were the two who resided just down the road in the White House. Although the Walshes and the McLeans found friendship in presidents Taft, Harding, Coolidge, and Hoover, it was President and Mrs. Warren G. Harding who came to be very close with Evalyn and Ned, vacationing with them, and even serving as the godparents to their daughter.

On a day in June 1932, I saw a dusty automobile truck roll slowly past my house. I saw the unshaven, tired faces of the men who were riding in it standing up. On the side of the truck was an expanse of white cloth on which was a legend, "BONUS ARMY." It was not lost on me that those men, passing any one of my big houses, would see in such rich shelters a kind of challenge—2020 was a mockery of their want. I could remember when those same men, with others, had been cheered as they marched down Pennsylvania Avenue. While I recalled those war-time parades, I was reading in the newspapers that the Bonus Army men were going hungry in Washington.

Evalyn Walsh McLean was a socialite if ever there was one. She was also, in her own way, a sort of pop culture icon of the era. Whether as a faithful supporter of law enforcement officers, as a columnist for the *Washington Times Herald*, or as the subject of other people's commentaries, she made her way into the news of the day and even into a Cole Porter song—"Anything Goes."

And in 1932, at the same time that she was dealing with her mother's passing, her failing marriage, and the financial decline of the *Washington Post,* came the news that the young son of Charles Lindbergh had been kidnapped. For over twenty years, Evalyn had lived with continual and credible threats of kidnapping and death against her own children. And so, in response to this news, her compassion and maternal instincts kicked into high gear. Though her attempt was admirable and motive pure, the record of this undertaking shows that she, by dealing with a member of the underworld in an effort to expose the underworld, was taken—both her trust and her fortune. Evalyn's loss was $135,000. A dollar figure could not be assessed to the Lindbergh's loss.

As with most of us, Evalyn's experiences brought to her a settled maturity. Though her personality remained, her perspective on any number of things did change. Evalyn's life was filled with great happiness and unique opportunities, wonderful friends and precious family memories. It was also filled with pain, heartache, and great loss, including two children—Vincent at age nine and Evie at age twenty-four.

She knew the extremes of life, and lived to tell about it. At 6:15 PM on April 24, 1947, heartbroken by her daughter's death and surrounded by beloved friends, Evalyn Walsh McLean succumbed to pneumonia and exited this world stage.

CINCINNATI POLICE
PRIVILEGE CARD
1941   No. 441
THE BEARER: Evalyn McLean
IS PRIVILEGED TO PASS
POLICE LINES; ACCOUNT   Cincinnati Enquirer
THIS PERMIT IS FOR USE BY THE PERSON TO WHOM ISSUED
PURPOSE APPROPRIATE TO HIS POSITION AS SHOWN. ANY ATTE
TO USE IT OTHERWISE WILL VOID THE PERMIT.
                    EUGENE T. WEATHERL
                    CHIEF OF POLICE
EXPIRES DECEMBER 31, 1941

People we read too much about . . . No. ?

Evalyn Walsh McLean . . . Indubitably, as they say, her ness, but her perennial talent for landing smack on the front reached a monotony. She's always been "good copy"—cavort Europe, Newport and Washington—getting engaged, diser finally married to Ned McLean—smuggling the 120,000- of the East into the States—buying the 154,000-dollar Hop for which she claims she was sued by Cartier for payment—monkey in her bathroom and a llama on her lawn—tossing lar dinner parties for lassoed celebrities. She says in her aut "The one continuing problem in my life . . . what amusin I do next?" Whatever it is, we'd rather read less about it.

GREAT DETECTIVE AND ARCH CRIMINAL

Gaston Means, America's Jekyll-Hyde, Near Death in Prison

On a white, narrow, iron bed in Leavenworth Penitentiary's two-story dust-bitten hospital building bulged the beefy frame of Gaston B. Means. America's one-time No. 1 sleuth nervously clenched the iron bed-frame while sweat drooped over his thick neck and heavy jaw.

In a corner of the ward, physicians debated on whether to operate on him. They knew that an operation might mean death.

Last week, Gaston Means toppled over a spittoon he was cleaning and fell to the floor with a cramp. Three years of confinement had weakened and undermined the once burly, 230-pound giant. Rushed to the hospital, he was diagnosed as having a severe kidney and bladder ailment.

If he recovers from his present illness, he will still have twelve more years to think over his stupendous law violations. High-lights of his astounding career include the charges: breach of promise, espionage, forgery, murder, opening of bonded warehouses of the Government to bootleggers, ninety-nine other violations of the National Prohibition Act, use of the mails to defraud, bribery to protect criminals, rifling the offices of United States Senators, larceny, embezzlement and conspiracy.

And yet, unlike nearly every criminal of his type and caliber, Gaston Means's record remained spotless during the first half of his life. Then, at the age of thirty-three, young Gaston was diligently developing his fantastic talents as a confidential man and investigator for J. W. Cannon, cotton-mill king, in whose North Carolina neighborhood the highly gifted detective had been born and reared.

His erudition first was applied when he took an insurance company over the hurdles for $4,000 in 1914.

The same year, the giant swaggered into the Burns Detective Agency. Within another year, he was rated as the greatest operative in that organization.

One morning, twelve months later,

him roughly $60,000 of her money within a few months.

A "second will" which he produced would turn over to Mrs. King the entire $6,000,000 estate, of which only $1,000,000 had been awarded to her. His commission he fixed at $950,000, payable when the courts declared the will valid.

But Mrs. King wanted to marry again, and this did not fit into handsome Gaston's plans. One night in August, 1917, he arranged a moonlight target-shooting party, together with two friends. Near Blackwelder Springs, North Carolina, the party left the automobile.

Means suddenly became thirsty, insisted on drinking from a forest spring. Mrs.

Acme

Gaston B. Means looks back on a record of spying, helping bootleggers, and hoax of $104,000 in the Lindbergh case

Story of Lindbergh Kidnaping A Series of Bizarre Incidents

No Case in Criminal History Aroused Such Interest—Countless Leads Followed in Effort to Find Murderer.

By EDMUND DE LONG.

The world was startled into incredulity on the night of March 1, 1932, when word came from the small town of Hopewell, N. J., that Charles A. Lindbergh Jr., son of the transatlantic flyer and Anne Morrow, had been stolen from his nursery crib.

I may spring from peasant stock, but that was a stirring, after years of luxury, of noblesse oblige. This is why I feel no chagrin whatever for having failed in an impossible undertaking. I am sorry that I failed, that I was tricked; but I shall always be glad that in my heart there was something that compelled me to try my best to take part in the effort to ransom the Lindbergh baby.

*O*nce, just before a snowy Christmas, a stream of threatening letters poured into the White House. A sort of final warning was delivered in which some mysterious enemy boasted that on Christmas Day the thing would happen. Mrs. Harding said to me, "Evalyn, we want to spend that day somewhere else." She was wearing at her throat a diamond buckle ornament that I had selected as her Christmas present the year before; it was excuse for a black velvet band that neatly hid her aging neck. "You come and stay with us," I said.

THIS BOOK contains a photographic record of some happy excursions in the south by land and water enjoyed by President and Mrs Warren G. Harding as guests of Mr and Mrs Edward B. McLean who were accompanied by their children. These sojourns began in nineteen hundred and twenty, when Mr Harding was elected President of the United States of America and continued through the years of his presidency until his untimely death on August the second Nineteen hundred and twenty three.

Outside of 2020 Massachusetts Avenue a blizzard wind was howling and the noise of it seemed to take the shape of words I'd heard about people starving and freezing in the parks. Alice Longworth was staying with me.

"Alice," I said, "I simply can't stand this. I am going out to investigate, to see just who is sleeping in the park with newspapers wrapped around them."

"Evalyn, you can't do that," said Alice.

"I can and I am; I am going

HARRY WINSTON
AND HIS GIFT OF HOPE

For the Hope, after centuries of existence, its life was in many ways, just getting started.

Harry Winston's seemingly innate talent for recognizing and enhancing the gems of this world was evident at a very early age. In order to hone this talent and to help out with the family jewel business, Winston dropped out of school at age fifteen. By the age of nineteen, he had opened his own store located at 535 Fifth Avenue in New York. His hard work and savvy business sense resulted in a thriving endeavor. In 1932 he formed Harry Winston, Inc.

Winston's basic philosophy was that diamonds, jewels of all kinds, were unique creatures, and should be treated as such. And though he dealt with the world of the financial elite, he also believed that people of all ages, backgrounds, and economic standing should be able to enjoy these treasures of the earth, and to understand and appreciate

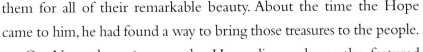

them for all of their remarkable beauty. About the time the Hope came to him, he had found a way to bring those treasures to the people.

On November 16, 1949, the Hope diamond was the featured guest at the Bal de Tete, a charity ball for the Veterans Music Service at the Ritz-Carlton Hotel. This was the beginning of what became known as Winston's Court of Jewels, a kaleidoscopic tour of glitz and glamour serving as the draw for a whole host of charitable events.

For four years, this collection of famous diamonds, featuring two of Evalyn's own—the Hope diamond and the Star of the East— would travel throughout the States and even to Cuba and Canada "wowing" and dazzling the masses. This was but a preview for the Hope's upcoming solo act—first when Winston continued to tour her without the help of the others, then on the stage where we now find her so majestically starring in her place of prominence. Harry Winston made this possible.

It was Winston's deep belief that the United States should have a national jewel collection of which we, as a nation, could be proud.

These Charming People

SOCIETY   SERVICE   PHOTOGRAFY

WOMEN'S CLUBS   TRAVEL

Times Herald

SUNDAY, OCT. 28, 1951

REG. U. S. PAT. OFFICE

Mrs. Jerauld Wright, wife of Vice Admiral Wright, U.S.N., models a necklace which has had many owners.

Mrs. George M. Ferris Jr. wears the famous Inquisition necklace. It once belonged to a Spanish grandee.

Mrs. A. S. Mike Monroney, wife of the Oklahoma senator, models a jewel as big as all out West— the fabulous Hope diamond.

Mrs. Alben W. Barkley, wife of the Vice President, wears the super-colossal Hope diamond, once owned by the late Mrs. Evalyn Walsh McLean, and is a dazzling blue stone.

PHOTOS BY

YORK, March 24.—(AP)—
ope diamond is going on a
wide tour for the benefit of
ational Foundation for Infan-
olysis.

eat blue diamond i
of jewelr
be

International Soundphoto

Famous McLean Gems Displayed in New York by New Owner

do and Grace Flynt admire the Evalyn Walsh
ewel collection recently acquired and displayed
by Harry Winston of New York. The Hope diamond is
shown on bust at left. At right is the Star of the East.

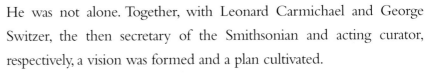

He was not alone. Together, with Leonard Carmichael and George Switzer, the then secretary of the Smithsonian and acting curator, respectively, a vision was formed and a plan cultivated.

It took nearly two years for all of the details to be hammered out. Finally, on November 10, 1958 a Christmas gift was delivered to the Smithsonian's Museum of Natural History. A plain brown package, sent from New York by way of the U.S. Postal Service, made its way to our nation's capital. Labeled specimen number 217868, this native of India became an American citizen, and one of history's greatest travelers took up a new and long-lasting residence.

THE HOPE AT CENTER STAGE

Since November 10, 1958, the Hope diamond has left the Smithsonian only four times.

For one month, in 1962, after some beaurocratic wrangling and some disentangling of red tape, the Hope was displayed with its fellow victims of crime—the Regent, the Sancy, and its Order of the Golden Fleece companion the red spinel dragon. Displayed together, these once scattered gems were reunited after one hundred and seventy years.

As part of the agreement between the Louvre and the Smithsonian, an exchange of equal benefit was required. In 1963, this promised exchange took place when a French national treasure boasting its own mystery and intrigue, and that with a certain lady and her famous

smile, embarked upon a voyage to America. The *Mona Lisa* was exhibited at the National Gallery of Art in Washington, D.C.

Since then, the Hope has journeyed to Johannesburg, South Africa for the 1965 Rand Easter Show. It was displayed, in 1982, at New York's Metropolitan Museum of Art for the 50th anniversary celebration of Harry Winston, Inc. Here our social diamond was again reunited with some old friends, as it was rejoined with the Star of the East and the Idol's Eye diamond (from the Court of Jewels fame) to dazzle the crowd. And lastly, in 1996 Harry Winston, Inc. decided our gem needed a fresh polish, and took some time to clean her up a bit and restore some faded brilliance.

On February 9, 2005, more than three centuries after King Louis XIV first laid his eyes on this treasure, the Smithsonian Institution published the findings of a detailed study, concluding that the Hope diamond is, in fact, part of the stolen French Crown jewels.

And on August 19, 2009, the Smithsonian Institution announced that the Hope diamond was to get a temporary new setting in celebration of a half-century at the National Museum of Natural History. In September of 2009, this stunning treasure was exhibited as a stand-alone gem with no setting, and on November 21, 2010 a new setting from Winston Jewelers, Inc.—Embracing Hope—was unveiled to the general public. Future plans are to return the Hope diamond to its most famous encasing, which was made so by its most famous owner.

For over three hundred years this gem has awed its audience, be it an audience of one or of millions. With charm and intrigue this great mystery of nature has captivated minds and hearts throughout the world—of kings and queens, of thieves and jewelers, the wealthy and poor alike.

HARRY WINSTON

Under the ownership of the citizens of the United States now for over fifty years, this beautiful diamond has found an honored place of residence in the Winston Gallery at the Smithsonian National Museum of Natural History. It seems a fitting home for this captivating natural wonder. No longer buried in obscurity within the earth, but simply and elegantly displayed in such a way that its rare qualities are given light and allowed to shine—and this for even the least among us to witness.

Now, nearly four hundred years since the "curse" took place, we find that this legendary eye of an idol has come to rest peacefully in a place where millions of eyes every year focus their attention on its remarkable beauty and reflect on its mystery and the myth that surrounds its long and adventurous life.

Like any precious gem, Evalyn Walsh McLean had flaws. With [?]
all her character defects, Evalyn's personality and life were
reflected in the fabulous Hope diamond. With it she captured the
attention of others, directing them toward what she thought was
"right" at the moment. Evalyn Walsh McLean lived in the present,
built on the past, and foresaw tremendous hope for the future.

*We live our span of allotted time and
then pass on to greater things. After all, we
are all treading the same road, and a few
months or a few years mean so little in the
eternity of time.*

Money is lovely to have . . .

. . . AND I HAVE LOVED HAVING IT, BUT
IT DOES NOT REALLY BRING THE BIG
THINGS OF LIFE—FRIENDS, HEALTH,
RESPECT—AND IT IS SO APT TO MAKE
ONE SOFT AND SELFISH. THE REAL THINGS,
I HAVE FOUND OUT, ARE QUIET AND
PEACE IN YOUR OWN SOUL, LOVE AND
THOUGHT FOR THE PEOPLE AROUND
YOU, AND, ABOVE ALL, THE CARE AND
DEVOTION YOU GIVE TO YOUR CHILDREN

For further investigation visit

www.evalynwalshmclean.com
www.fable-hdc.com

ILLUSTRATIONS

Unless otherwise noted, photographic images are found in the Public Domain. Additional images are noted as follows: The private collection of Joseph Gregory (JG); Smithsonian Institution © 2010 (SI); Library of Congress (LOC); Creative Commons Attribution 2.0 Generic (CC 2.0); Creative Commons Attribution Share Alike 2.5 Generic (CC 2.5); Creative Commons Attribution Share Alike 3.0 (CC 3.0); Creative Commons Attribution 3.0 Unported (CC 3.0 U); Winston Jewelers, Inc. (WJI). Additional images provided courtesy of Kathrine Currey (KC).

Page	Description

Page	Description

ABOUT THE AUTHOR

Joseph Gregory is the great-grandson of Evalyn Walsh McLean. Originally from Louisville, Kentucky, he was educated at Belmont University in Nashville, Tennessee. He is the founder and president of Hope Diamond Collection Inc., which has created and marketed a fragrance called Fable, inspired by his great-grandmother's legendary life and legacy. Gregory travels around the world to formally speak about both the Hope diamond and the earlier re-release of his great-grandmother's successful autobiography, *Queen of Diamonds*. As the unofficial McLean family historian, his travels give him the opportunity to share how the Hope diamond has colored his life and that of his family. Future plans for Gregory include a third book to be released in conjunction with a touring museum exhibit featuring his great-grandmother's personal belongings. He lives and works in Nashville, New York, and Florida.